THE GREEN DETECTIVE

IN THE WARDROBE

Clothes and the Environment

ANGELA GRUNSELL

Wayland

The Green Detective...

... at the Chemist	... at the Newsagent
... up the Chimney	... on the Road
... down the Drains	... at the Takeaway
... in the Kitchen	... in the Wardrobe

The Green Detective investigates different aspects of environmental problems, relating them to everyday activities. The table is a guide to the issues covered in each title.

	Up The Chimney	In The Kitchen	Down The Drains	At The Newsagent	At The Chemist	At The Takeaway	On The Road	In The Wardrobe
Air pollution	✔			✔	✔		✔	
Water pollution		✔	✔	✔	✔			✔
Loss of habitats	✔	✔	✔	✔	✔	✔	✔	✔
Animal welfare		✔			✔	✔		✔
Food production	✔	✔				✔		
Personal health		✔	✔		✔	✔		
Energy use	✔	✔		✔		✔	✔	✔
Waste and recycling	✔	✔	✔	✔	✔	✔	✔	✔
World poverty		✔	✔		✔	✔		✔

Editing and picture research: Paul Bennett & Associates, Tonbridge

Series design: Carr Associates Graphics, Brighton

Series consultant: Stephen Sterling, independent environmental consultant

First published in 1992 by
Wayland (Publishers) Ltd
61 Western Road, Hove
East Sussex, BN3 1JD, England

© Copyright 1992 Wayland (Publishers) Ltd

British Library Cataloguing in Publication Data

Grunsell, Angela
  Green Detective in the Wardrobe
  I. Title
  687
  ISBN 0-7502-0323-4

Typeset by Paul Bennett & Associates, Tonbridge
Printed in Italy by Rotolito Lombarda S.p.A., Milan
Bound in Belgium by Casterman S.A.

Contents

Words printed in **bold** can be
found in the glossary on
page 30.

Becoming a green detective

There are many things
you can do to help
save our planet – this is
what being 'green' is all about.
Why not start by becoming a 'green detective'?
Ask questions and gather some evidence. Then you can find out what
damage is being done to the Earth and how you can help to stop it.
Remember – like a real detective, you don't always have to believe
everything you are told. You can make up your own mind.

You might think that your actions can't possibly have any effect on our
planet. Once you start investigating, you might find you are wrong. Most
environmental problems are linked together in very complicated ways –
but they are all caused by people. They can be solved by people too.
What you do can really make a difference.

What's in your wardrobe?

When you open the door of your wardrobe, do you ever wonder about your clothes? Where did they all come from? What are they made out of? Who made them?

Clothes are one of our basic needs. They keep us warm in winter and cool in summer. They protect us from the sun, wind, rain and snow.

Clothes are big business too. Shoppers spend millions of pounds on new clothes every year, and most high streets have more clothes shops than anything else. Throughout the world, millions of people are employed in producing material and making it into shoes, trainers, coats, shirts, vests, skirts and trousers.

Knowing about our clothes is an important part of being green, because the clothing industry affects everyone's **environment**.

Look at the clothes in your wardrobe, and ask yourself some questions about them. Become a green detective and start investigating!

Who sewed this cotton T-shirt?

How much did these fashionable trainers cost?

How were the T-shirts dyed these colours?

Where was this cotton grown?

What kind of fabric are these clothes made from?

Who chose this coat?

What are these boots made from?

How is waterproof nylon made?

Looking good

Which of your clothes do you most like wearing? Why?

Everyone enjoys putting on their favourite clothes – they help to make you feel more confident and attractive.

Clothes are also a way of saying something about yourself. You might choose to wear casual clothes if you want to look relaxed, for example. Some people spend a lot of time and money on keeping up with ever-changing **fashions**.

Clothes shops and manufacturers need to encourage people to buy clothes. Advertisements in magazines or on television show good-looking and successful people wearing the latest clothes. The advertisements can have an effect on the way we feel about our clothes.

Can you remember an advertisement for trainers that you have seen recently? What makes you want to buy certain trainers and not others?

Fashions in 1980 (left) and 1992. What we think looks good today will look strange and old fashioned in ten years' time.

YOU INVESTIGATE

The best way to start investigating clothes is to make a survey of your own wardrobe.

1. First, count how many T-shirts, trousers, skirts, socks, vests, trainers and other clothes you have.
2. Then make a list of all the clothes you have in your wardrobe. Ask yourself a set of questions about each item of clothing, and make a chart like the one below:

Item	What is it made of?	When did I buy it?	When did I last wear it?	Has the brand or make been advertised?
T-shirt	Cotton	May	August	No
Jeans	Cotton	January	September	Yes
Blue dress	Viscose	June	June	Yes
Anorak	Nylon, polyester and cotton	August	September	No
Socks	Polyester and cotton	May	October	N
Scarf	Wool	October	November	

Are you surprised by the amount of clothes you have in your wardrobe? Do you think you need them all?

Clothes from animal skins

The very first clothes were animal skins. Early humans hunted animals and used the hairy or furry coats to keep themselves warm.

If you wear leather or fur, you probably won't have killed the animal it came from yourself, but animal skins are still an important way of making clothes. A lot of shoes are made of leather – animal hide that has been smoothed and specially treated. And some people still like to wear fur coats to keep themselves warm.

Nearly all of the fur that you see in clothes shops nowadays comes from fur farms. There, animals that are valued for their fur, such as chinchillas or mink, are reared until they are ready to be killed.

The leg-hold trap. For animals that don't get strangled, beaten, gassed or electrocuted.

Poster campaigns like this one have persuaded many people that it is wrong to buy and wear clothes made from animal fur.

FACT BOX

The Kayapo Amerindians live in Brazil. Many still follow a very simple, traditional way of life in the Amazon rainforest. They are hunters but also have a very respectful attitude towards the plants and animals around them. If they killed too many animals, their own supply of food and clothing would run out, so they have strict rules about hunting. They use every part of anything that they kill.

These Kayapo hunters are following a traditional way of life.

However, some rare species of animal are still hunted in the wild for their skins. For these **endangered species**, hunting is a threat to their existence. In recent years, governments, encouraged by organizations such as Greenpeace have made new laws to stop the hunting. But many rare animals are still killed every year for their coats.

The **poaching** of endangered species is a difficult problem to overcome. In South America, the Caiman Jacare alligator is hunted for its skin, which can be used to make shoes or handbags.

In Paraguay and Brazil, alligator hunting is banned altogether. In some other countries, hunting is allowed, but there is a strict control on the number of alligators that may be killed, so that they do not become **extinct**.

The Caiman Jacare alligator is now an endangered species. Its skin has been made into expensive items, such as shoes, wallets and cases.

However, controlled hunting provides only one-third of the demand for alligator skins, and poaching is a serious problem. For some poor people in South America, killing alligators is the only way of making the money they need to feed their families – even though they run the risk of being arrested or shot.

Poachers sell the alligator skins to organized gangs of criminals, who bribe and threaten officials and smuggle the skins out of South America. The skins are then smuggled to Europe, where manufacturers are willing to pay a high price for them.

Can you understand the problems facing governments that try to stop the hunting of endangered species? Can you think of anything else we could do to protect animals such as the Caiman Jacare alligator?

YOU INVESTIGATE

People have very different attitudes towards wearing clothes made from the skins of animals. Some people will not wear anything at all that is made from an animal skin. Others object to killing rare species, but are happy to wear fur clothes from a fur farm. Other people may not wear furs, but think that it is all right to wear leather, which can be made from the hides of animals that have died naturally or have been used for meat.

Fur and leather questionnaire				
Question	Mum	Dad	Ahmed	Selma
Do you think people should kill animals to clothe themselves?	Yes	No	Yes	No
Would you wear a real fur or leather coat?	Yes	Yes	Yes	No
Do you buy and wear real leather shoes?	Yes	Yes	Yes	Yes
Do you have a leather coat?	No	Yes	Yes	No
Do you have a fur coat?	Yes	No	No	

You could make a fur and leather questionnaire. Then ask your friends and family what they think about wearing fur and leather. Which animal-skin products are people least willing to wear?

Cotton

Cotton is an excellent clothing material. It is a strong, long-lasting fibre, produced by the cotton plant. It is comfortable to wear because it absorbs sweat. It has been grown and used by people in many parts of the world for about 5,000 years.

How cotton is produced

The fibres are then packed together in large bales.

When ripe, the cotton plant head (or boll) splits open, and the fluffy cotton fibres burst out and dry in the sun.

The cotton seeds are seperated from the fibres by a machine called a gin.

The cotton plants are harvested, either by hand or by a mechanical harvester.

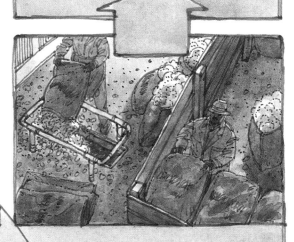

The cotton is unloaded ready for the seeds to be removed from the fibres.

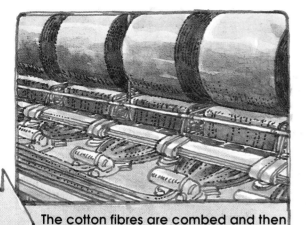

The cotton fibres are combed and then spun to make them into thread.

The finished cloth is ready to be cut and sewn together into an item of clothing.

Using a loom, the cotton threads are woven to make a piece of cloth.

The cloth is bleached to remove its natural yellowish colour. It can then be dyed.

The different parts of the cotton plant have many uses.

SEED HUSK used for:
Cattle feed
Flour

LINT used for:
Bandages
Book-binding
Clothing
Sheets and towels
Typing ribbon
Umbrellas

SEED KERNEL used for:
Cooking oil
Margarine
Soap

FUZZY LINTERS used for:
Clear tape
Explosives
Ice-cream
Lino
Mattress stuffing
Mops
Nail varnish
Paint
Photographic film
Records
Sausage skins
Shampoo
Toothpaste
Wallpaper

STEM ploughed back into soil to improve it.

13

A cotton field in Sudan. Food crops could be grown on the irrigated land.

Cotton is grown in about eighty countries across the world. Some of the countries that grow cotton, such as the USA, are wealthy **developed countries**.

But many of the cotton-growing areas are in poor countries, such as the Sudan. (These poor countries are in what is sometimes called the **Third World**, or The South.) Some of them have been providing cheap raw materials for Europe ever since they were made into **colonies** by European countries over one hundred years ago.

Today, most poor nations are **independent**, but they still need money to build houses, schools and hospitals, or to pay off large loans that they have borrowed from the rich countries of the world. Cotton is important to them because it is a **cash crop**. Selling cotton to wealthy countries is often one of the few ways that poor countries can make much needed money.

In some poor countries, landowners may choose to use the land for cash crops rather than food crops, even if there is not enough food for all the people.

Many of the poor cotton-growing countries, such as Bangladesh, also make cloth and finished cotton clothes. There, the workers are paid extremely low wages even though they work long hours. Children and young women are often employed in the clothes factories.

In Western Europe and North America, people can buy a T-shirt for less than the cost of a cinema ticket or a take-away pizza. Yet the people who have made the T-shirt may hardly be able to afford to buy one decent meal a day.

FACT BOX

Charities and organizations, such as Traidcraft, support projects which pay higher wages to clothes makers. They buy directly from clothes producers, pay a fair price and share out any profit from sales among them.

The charity, OXFAM, supports Thea, a project in the Philippines that provides training and work for sixty women, and also loans to buy sewing machines. The clothes are sold through OXFAM's mail order catalogue.

The Thea project in the Philippines.

Synthetics

Did you find many clothes in your wardrobe made from materials such as viscose, nylon, Terylene or polyester? These are **synthetic** materials and are made from **chemicals**. The chemicals themselves come from all sorts of sources. They are found in air and water, or in vegetable products, such as oats, wood pulp and even waste cotton. Most important, synthetics need chemicals from fossil fuels – oil and coal.

Synthetic fibres have many advantages. They are both light and waterproof. They can be washed at low temperatures, and come clean easily because dirt does not stick to them as much as it does to cotton or wool. Synthetics also dry more quickly than natural fibres, and often they do not need ironing.

However, there is a drawback to synthetic fibres. The coal and oil that they use is a **non-renewable resource**. Coal and oil are found beneath

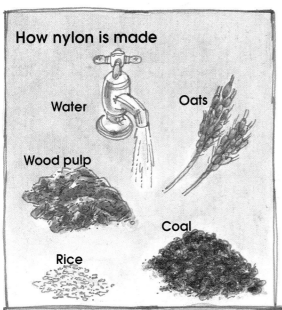

Chemicals are made from such things as water, coal, oats, wood pulp and coal.

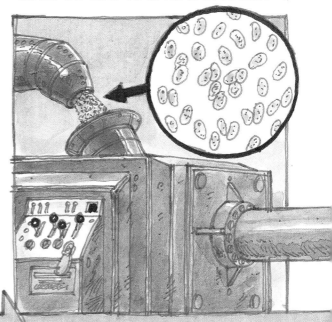

The chemicals are mixed together and formed into small white shapes which are then melted .

the earth, where they took millions of years to form. However, there is only a limited amount of oil and coal in the ground, and one day our supplies will run out. So, eventually, we will no longer have the chemicals to make synthetic materials.

Natural fibres are a **renewable resource**. Providing that humans use the land sensibly, they will always be able to grow cotton and use reared animals for their wool and their skins.

... and wound on to a reel or bobbin.

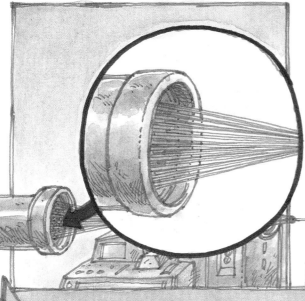

The liquid is pushed through the tiny holes of a machine called a spinneret. The jets of liquid are dried and a piece of nylon thread is formed.

The threads are stretched on rollers to become nylon yarn ...

Wool

Like cotton, wool is one of the oldest natural clothing materials. It feels warm, and is wind proof, and partly waterproof.

Wool comes not only from sheep, but also from many other animals who live in the cooler, upland areas of the world. Angora rabbits, llamas and goats all have the kind of fur we call wool.

Wool is a great green choice. You do not have to kill animals to collect their wool. Shearing sheep is rather like a hair cut – it doesn't hurt, and the wool soon grows back again. Sheep are sheared in the spring and summer when they no longer need their coats to keep warm.

Sheep and goats can live on high and steep land which cannot be used for growing crops. However, they are greedy eaters,

Farmers shear their sheep in the spring and summer. People have made clothes from wool for thousands of years.

18

and it is important to control where they are allowed to graze. If too many animals graze on a piece of land for too long, they will eat all the vegetation, so that there is nothing to protect the soil. The soil may then be **eroded** away.

In the past, overgrazing has caused the destruction of forests in many parts of Europe, especially in dry regions such as Spain. Today, overgrazing is also a problem in other dry areas, such as India and North Africa. People are now recognizing the importance of maintaining a careful balance between the different needs of animals, people and the planet. Everywhere, people are learning about the need to control where animals graze.

Sheep grazing in a British wood. They are eating the shoots of the new trees before they have a chance to grow.

How green are natural fibres?

To kill the pests that live in the wool of sheep, farmers dip the sheep in poisonous chemicals. Unfortunately, the chemicals find their way into streams and rivers, and kill the plants and animals that live there.

Chemicals that kill insect pests are sprayed on to cotton plants. These **pesticides** give off a gas, carbon dioxide, which harms the **ozone layer**. The pesticides are also harmful to people – it is estimated that 20,000 people die from pesticide poisoning every year. Manufacturers and scientists are working to find less dangerous and harmful ways of protecting sheep and crops.

Many fabrics, including those made from wool and cotton, are bleached to make them white. To do this, chemicals such as chlorine are used. Chlorine is highly poisonous but,

Women workers in a co-operative – a business where profits are shared – in India. They are using natural dyes to colour cotton cloth.

These fish have been killed by pesticides. Rivers and streams near to farms can become polluted by the chemicals that are sprayed on the crops.

despite this, some factories **discharge** waste chlorine into rivers where it kills fish and other wildlife.

The bleached fabric can be coloured using chemicals called aniline dyes, liquids that are also poisonous to the environment.

Friends of the Earth, and other organizations concerned with the environment, are now importing and selling unbleached cotton garments. Unbleached T-shirts look attractive and eye-catching. If we start wanting to buy them, manufacturers will quickly start to produce these T-shirts and other unbleached clothes.

Colours produced by natural dyes are often more attractive than the harsh colours produced by chemical dyes. On the next page you can find out how to colour a fabric using natural dyes.

Y🔍U INVESTIGATE

For hundreds of years, before the development of modern chemical dyes, people used vegetable dyes to colour their clothes. With the help of an adult, you can make your own vegetable dyes. Try a dye made from onion skins first, and then experiment with some other dyes.

3. Heat up the contents of the pan, and simmer for about two hours. Ask an adult to help you while you are using the cooker.

1. Collect enough brown onion skins to fill a large paper bag.

4. Put about 450 g of raw sheep's wool or white Aran wool in the pan along with the onion skins. Simmer for a further hour.

2. Put the onion skins in a large pan of water.

5. Take the pan off the heat and leave to cool. Then take out the wool and rinse it in clean warm water.

After a few days, wash your wool. Does the colour fade? To fix the colours of your wool, you should treat the wool before dyeing it. To do this, find a pan that is not made out of aluminium. Simmer the wool for 45 minutes along with 75g of alum, which you can buy from the chemist. Take the wool off the heat and leave to cool. You can store the wool for up to a week in a plastic bag in the fridge, until you are ready to dye it.

Once you have tried making a dye from onion skins, you can experiment with other natural dyes. You can try:
• elderberries
• dandelions
• tea bags
• nettles (make sure you always wear gloves when you handle nettles).

Make a chart to show the results of your experiments.

Dye ingredient	Colour of ingredient	Colour of dyed wool
Onion skin	Brown	Biege to deep chestnut
Elderberry		
Dandelion		
Tea bag		
Nettle		
Blackberries		
Beetroot		

Recycling clothes

By selling second-hand clothes, charity shops can raise a lot of money.

What do you do with your clothes when they have worn out, or you have grown out of them? Do you simply throw them in the dustbin, or have you thought of ways they could be reused?

There are lots of ways of **recycling** clothes. If something does not fit any more, it could perhaps be used by someone else. You could hand on your old clothes to a younger member of the family, or give the clothing to a charity shop.

Many charities have charity shops. Some people feel embarrassed about the idea of buying clothes in these shops. They worry that other people might look down on them, or think they are poor.

But second-hand clothes are a good way of reusing resources, helping charities and adding to your own wardrobe without spending a lot of money.

Even if your clothes have become too old and tatty to be used by anybody else, it may still be possible

FACT BOX

Clothes are a basic human need. Not everyone can always meet this basic need for themselves. They may be caught up in a war or a natural disaster, such as a flood or earthquake.

OXFAM started during the Second World War when a group of people started collecting clothes to send to refugee children in Greece.

They were given so many clothes that they also decided to open the first charity shop, to raise money that they could send to the victims of disasters at home and overseas.

Sending clothes to people in emergencies is still an important part of OXFAM's work. It always keeps a stock of clothes packed ready to send abroad in emergencies.

In 1991, many Kurdish people who were under attack in Iraq fled from their homes into the mountains. Charities sent warm clothing to save their lives.

to recycle the material from which the clothes are made. In the north of England, OXFAM runs a Wastesaver plant – the largest centre for recycling clothes in Europe. It recycles over 8,000 tonnes of cloth every year.

Wastesaver proves that it is possible to recycle cloth. In the future, it could become much more common to make clothes from recycled material, instead of using up more new resources.

The clothes are sorted at high speed by highly skilled textile sorters. They divide the clothes into thirty different grades of cloth.

Unwanted clothes are packed into black bags by charity shop volunteers. Most sorts of fabric can be recycled, but small garments such as underwear or ties, and rubber or foam-backed materials cannot be treated by Wastesaver.

The old clothes are collected and driven to the Wastesaver factory in Bradford.

A machine, made in Italy, bales the different kinds of cloth. The bales of cloth are loaded on to lorries ready for delivering to customers.

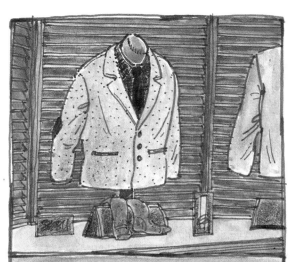

3. Good quality cloth can be recycled to make certain kinds of new fabric. Tweed, a material often used for men's jackets, is made out of recycled cloth. Wool too can be recycled, especially if it is white and can easily be dyed another colour.

The recycled cloth has one of three uses...

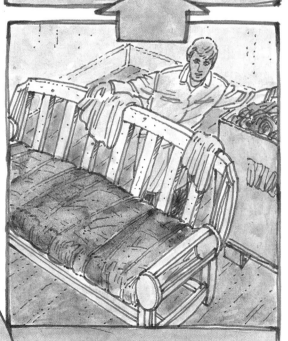

1. Cloth can be used as wiping rags by industry. It may be used for cleaning machinery in factories.

2. Cloth can be used as stuffing for furniture and in the cushions of chairs and settees.

Green choices

Making green choices isn't always easy. As the investigations in this book have shown, the facts about our clothes – where they came from and how they were made – are often very complicated.

You may decide that you do not want to wear fur because it is an animal skin. But then you have to remember that synthetic fibres also use up valuable natural resources of oil and coal.

However, many people are now much more aware about green issues when they go shopping for new clothes – and our green choices are increasing all the time. Designers are using more and more natural dyes and unbleached cotton.

Charities, and even some large companies, are supporting projects where clothes workers can work in safe conditions for fairer pay. And scientists are developing environmentally friendly fabrics made, for example, from banana and pineapple fibres.

From what you know about synthetic clothing, do you think they are an ideal green choice?

You too can influence the kind of clothes that are produced and sold in the shops. As as consumer, you choose how and where to spend your money. Advertisements may try to persuade you to buy certain kinds of clothes, but the final decision is yours.

And you can decide to make green choices. In the end, if more people want to buy green clothing for their wardrobes, shops and companies will have to start producing it.

YOU DECIDE

Using the information in this book, you could make a fact sheet for each different kind of material in your wardrobe. Write down what you think are the advantages of a type of material, and balance them out against the disadvantages.

Balance sheet for cotton

Facts	Advantages	Disadvantages	What I can do
Cotton is a natural fibre which comes from a plant.

It needs plenty of heat, sunshine and water to grow. | It is a renewable resourse because new plants can be grown every year.

It is comfortable to wear because it absorbs sweat.

It is long lasting and strong. | It is sometimes grown on land which could be used to produce food.

Pesticides and fertilizers which damage the environment are used on the crops.

It is often bleached using harmful chemicals.

Many cotton workers are paid very low wages. | Buy unbleached cotton T-shirts.

Buy clothing from 'fair trade' organisations such as Traidcraft.

Find out c campaign for minir wages |

Glossary

Cash crop A crop that is grown to be sold, and not to be eaten or used by the farmer's family.

Chemicals Substances that are formed by or used in a chemical process. Chemistry is the study of the substances and the ways in which they join together or react with each other.

Colonies Countries under the rule of other countries.

Developed countries Those countries that earn most of their money through industry. They incluse the USA, Canada, the countries of Europe, Australia, New Zealand and Japan.

Discharge To release or set free something into the environment.

Endangered species A group of plants or animals that are at risk of becoming extinct.

Environment The surroundings that humans, animals and plants live in. The environment includes the·air, water and soil.

Eroded Soil or rock that has been worn away, usually by the action of wind or water.

Extinct When the last of a species of animals or plants dies, that type of animal or plant becomes extinct. For example, dinosaurs and mammoths are now extinct.

Fashions Clothes that are the latest style of dress.

Independent Countries that are free to rule themselves.

Ozone layer A layer of gas found in the atmosphere. It filters out some of the harmful rays from the sun.

Pesticides Chemicals used to kill insects that attack crops.

Poaching Where fish are caught or animals are hunted illegally.

Renewable resource A valuable resource used by people and industry that can be restored or put back in some way. For example, we can keep up stocks of wood by growing more trees.

Synthetic Something that humans have made and that is not found in nature.

Third World The countries of Africa, Asia and Latin America that are far less industrialized than the developed countries. Third World countries are also known as developing countries.

Further information

Books to read
Clothes and Fashion by Joanne Jessop (Wayland, 1991)
Costumes and Clothes by T. Rowland-Entwistle (Wayland, 1986)
Exploring Clothes by Brenda Ralph Lewis (Wayland, 1988)
Wool by Anabelle Dixon (A & C Black, 1988)
The Young Green Consumer Guide by John Elkinton and Julia Hailes
(Gollancz, 1988)

See also titles in Wayland's 'Our Clothes' series:
Denim Jeans, Leather Shoes, Nylon Tracksuit, Plastic Raincoat and
Woolly Hat

Teachers' resources
ALARO by OXFAM (an activity pack based on textiles from Nigeria)
Hanging by a Thread. Trade, Debt and Cotton in Tanzania by Leeds
Development Education Centre at 151 Cardigan Road, Leeds LS6 1LZ
An Early Start to Technology by Ray Richards (Simon and Schuster, 1990)

Useful addresses
British Clothing Industry Association
7 Swallow Place
London W1R 7AA

Community Aid Abroad
156 George Street
Fitzroy
Victoria 3065
Australia

Lynx
PO Box 300
Nottingham NG1 5HN

Lynx USA
Suite 155
10573 West Pico Boulevard
Los Angeles
California 90064

OXFAM
274 Banbury Road
Oxford OX27 7DZ

OXFAM Canada
Suite 301
251 Larier Avenue West
Ottawa
Ontario K1P 556

OXFAM USA
115 Broadway
Massachusetts 02116

Traidcraft
Team Valley Trading Estate
Gateshead NE11 0NE

Index

Picture acknowledgements

The photographs in this book were supplied by the following: Chapel Studios 20, 28; Bruce Coleman Ltd 10 (L C Marigo), 21 (Michael Price); Eye Ubiquitous 14 (Helene Rogers); Lynx 8; Marion and Tony Morrison 9 (Bill Leimbach); The National Trust 19; OXFAM 15 (Gil Nartea), 24 Camilla (Garrett-Jones); Topham 6 (left), 25; Wayland Picture Library *cover*; Tim Woodcock 6 (right). All artwork by Carr Associates Graphics.